GROSSER GOODIES

Beastly Bites That Look Bad But Taste Good

Tina Vilicich-Solomon

Illustrated by Neal Yamamoto

LOWELL HOUSE JUVENILE

LOS ANGELES

NTC/Contemporary Publishing Group

*For my dad—I shall always remember your culinary words of wisdom:
"Food should be fun, cooking creative, and eating . . . an experience!"
Thanks for being both friend and father forever and always. I love you.*
—T. V. S.

Published by Lowell House
A division of NTC/Contemporary Publishing Group, Inc.
4255 West Touhy Avenue, Lincolnwood (Chicago), Illinois 60646-1975 U.S.A.
Copyright © 1998 by NTC/Contemporary Publishing Group, Inc.

Managing Director and Publisher: Jack Artenstein
Director of Publishing Services: Rena Copperman
Editorial Director, Juvenile: Brenda Pope-Ostrow
Director of Juvenile Development: Amy Downing
Typesetting: Treesha Runnells
Cover Art: Dianne O'Quinn Burke

ISBN: 1-56565-734-9

Library of Congress Catalog Card Number: 98-66660

Lowell House books can be purchased at special discounts when ordered in bulk for
premiums and special sales. Please contact Customer Service at:

NTC/Contemporary
4255 W. Touhy Avenue
Lincolnwood, IL 60646
1-800-323-4900

Printed and bound in the United States of America
10 9 8 7 6 5 4 3 2 1

Contents

Before You Bake

*G*rosser Goodies contains all the ideas and kitchen help every budding gross gourmand needs to know. You'll find loads of recipes that are fun to make and even more fun to serve.

Get off to a good start by learning on the following pages important cooking terms as well as safety tips. When you see a recipe you'd like to make, read through it before you begin. Then gather all the ingredients and tools.

For some kitchen tools, such as measuring cups, take care to use the proper type. Liquids pour easily and accurately with a liquid-measuring cup. Be sure to check the measurements at eye level. Dry ingredients should be measured using stackable dry-measuring cups. Level them off using a spatula or butter knife for exact measuring. Because almost every recipe calls for measuring tools of some kind, measuring cups and measuring spoons have not been included under "Tools You'll Need." Always keep a selection handy.

Also, when required, be sure to prepare any tools properly, such as greasing your baking sheet. Place a small amount of butter or shortening on the baking sheet and thinly spread it over the surface using a clean paper towel, or simply coat the surface with nonstick cooking spray. In either case, if the recipe calls for a greased pan, it is important to coat the pan's entire surface so that food doesn't stick when baking.

Many recipes suggest microwave cooking instructions. Microwaves can vary in their cooking times, depending on their size and power. This book suggests cooking times based on the most commonly used power levels, 600 to 650 watts. If you're trying a recipe for the first time, be sure to check for doneness at regular intervals while heating any food item. If you do not have access to a microwave, alternate cooking suggestions are given. However, they will require different

5

cooking tools, so be sure to go over the recipe with an adult first.

All the recipes have been kitchen-tested and tasted and are wholly suitable for anyone who loves to eat good food—even if it does happen to look like doggy doo-doo! Dig in!

A BAKER'S DOZEN RULES
TO SURVIVE BY

1 Always have an adult help you when using the oven or stove, or any electrical appliance.

2 Read through your recipe thoroughly to make sure you have all the necessary ingredients and tools and enough time to prepare it.

3 Dress the part! Tie back long hair, fold up shirt sleeves, and wear an apron or old shirt over your clothes.

4 An adult should always be supervising when you are using knives or scissors.

5 Keep a fire extinguisher in your kitchen and know how to use it.

6 Wash your hands thoroughly before cooking and frequently as you handle various foods and utensils.

7 Turn saucepan handles to the side so they won't get knocked off the stove. Lift saucepan lids away from your face to avoid steam burns.

8 Have an adult check over your kitchen tools. Dull knives cause far more accidents than sharp ones, so be sure yours are in good condition!

9 Never leave the kitchen when something is cooking on the stove top.

10 Keep food safe from bacteria. Start with clean counters and tools. Keep refrigerated foods chilled until you're ready to use them. Never place cooked foods or foods that will be eaten raw on surfaces or in containers that held raw meats or eggs. Always refrigerate uneaten foods as soon as possible.

11 Always use thick, dry pot holders to handle hot pans, pots, baking sheets, or baking dishes.

12 Check all ingredients for freshness before using by sniffing them and examining them for mold or spoilage. Ask a parent to help you.

13 When you're finished preparing your creations, clean the kitchen and wash all the tools you used. This way you're sure to be welcomed back into the kitchen for a repeat performance as "the Ghastly Gourmand."

WORDS TO KNOW

baking sheet - a flat pan with no sides on it, designed for even heating of items, such as cookies

boil - to heat a liquid to the point where air bubbles form at the bottom of the pan

candy "eyes" - made from hard sugar, these candies are available in many sizes at cake-decorating supply stores and many craft supply stores

colander - a bowl with tiny holes used for washing and draining food

confectionery coating (also called candy-making chocolate) - a chocolate designed to stay smooth and evenly textured when melted

cutting board - a plastic mat or wooden block designed to protect countertops from damage while chopping or cutting

dash - a very slight addition of an ingredient, such as one sprinkle

divided - when an ingredient is separated into smaller amounts and added at different times

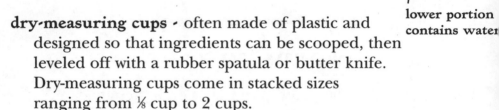

upper portion for ingredients

double boiler - a double saucepan designed to be filled with water in the lower portion and cooking ingredients in the upper portion. The heated water warms food slowly, preventing it from burning.

lower portion contains water

dry-measuring cups - often made of plastic and designed so that ingredients can be scooped, then leveled off with a rubber spatula or butter knife. Dry-measuring cups come in stacked sizes ranging from ⅛ cup to 2 cups.

electric mixer - an electrical appliance, often handheld, that's designed to mix ingredients quickly. Note: If you don't have one, most recipes can be mixed by hand with a wooden spoon, whisk, or heavy-duty rubber spatula.

fold - to combine light ingredients gently, such as whipped cream, with heavier ingredients, such as fruit, with minimal mixing

handheld bottle opener - a small tool about 4 inches long, with a pointed end for poking holes in cans and a rounded end for popping tops from bottles

heat-safe work surface - a work surface that is either protected from heat with a pot holder or is naturally resistant to heat

invert - to flip over and empty a pan or tray onto another surface, such as a cake plate or cutting board

jimmie cake-decorating sprinkles - tiny, hot-dog-shaped decorating candies, most often sprinkled over baked goods (available in single colors, mixed colors, or chocolate)

knead - to smooth and mix dough by folding it over and over using your hands and knuckles

line - to cover the interior of a baking sheet, pan, or bowl with removable protection, such as waxed paper or plastic wrap

liquid-measuring cup - usually made of clear plastic or glass and designed with a spout for pouring liquid measurements

microwave-safe container - container made of glass, plastic, or paper, safe for use in the microwave. (Never use metal, metal-trimmed, Styrofoam®, or handblown glass containing air bubbles.)

mix - to blend ingredients evenly by either stirring or beating

mixing bowl - a bowl that is deep enough for electric beaters to fit in without splattering ingredients over the sides. (Mixing bowls come in a variety of sizes.)

nonpareils - tiny candy balls available in many colors for sprinkling on baked goods

paring knife - a small, sharp knife with a short, narrow blade used for slicing and carving

peel - the outer skin of fruit or vegetables, or the action of removing the outer skin from fruit or vegetables

rubber spatula - a flat rubber tool with a long handle and flexible tip, used for scraping bowls and evenly spreading ingredients, such as frosting

serrated knife - a knife with jagged teeth much like those on a saw, best used for cutting dry items like bread

set - when ingredients, such as gelatin, are firm and solid throughout

sieve - a bowl-shaped utensil with a handle and fine-mesh interior used for separating solid foods from liquid or semiliquid ingredients

tongs - a tool used for picking up or turning hot items while cooling or dipping

utility knife - a 6- to 8-inch knife with a smooth, sharp blade

whisk - to whip or mix ingredients using a wire tool, also called a whisk

wooden spoon - a spoon made of wood used for stirring and mixing

NASTY
NIBBLES

Cat Food Pâté
on Toast
(page 18)

Chilled
Eyeballs
(page 20)

Potato
Bug Bits
(page 22)

FLUFFY

Eye Boogers

Eyes sealed tight with crusty boogers? Don't despair!
Rub your peepers over a platter and harvest those crunchy
pale green treats to serve to your friends.

INGREDIENTS

½ cup sugar

¼ cup water

¼ teaspoon almond extract

yellow and green food coloring

3 cups mini marshmallows

TOOLS YOU'LL NEED
• small mixing bowl • fork • waxed paper
• clean spray bottle

1 Place the sugar into a small mixing bowl and blend together with a fork. Lay two sheets of waxed paper (each about 12 inches long) side by side on your work surface.

2 Pour water and almond extract into a spray bottle. (Use a new spray bottle for cooking— *never use one that's been used for cleaning products*.) Add two drops yellow food coloring and one drop of green. Attach spray top to bottle and gently shake to blend colors.

3 Spread about ½ cup mini marshmallows onto one sheet of the waxed paper. Lightly but completely mist them with your water-filled spray bottle. Turn them over and mist the bottoms.

4 Pick up a small handful of moistened mini marshmallows and drop them into the sugar to create larger-than-life crusty eye boogers. Roll them with your fingers to coat evenly, then place them on the second sheet of waxed paper to dry. Repeat with remaining ingredients.

5 After about one hour, turn them over so that the eye boogers can dry evenly on all sides. These get more chewy with age, so if you're planning a party, you can make them a day or two ahead and store them, lightly covered, at room temperature.

Serves: 8 sleepy eaters (¼ rounded cup for each)

FREAKY FACT:

Real eye boogers begin life as lubricating moisture for your eyes, more commonly referred to as tears. Not only are they made of water, but they also contain albumin, ammonia, citric acid, salts, sugar, urea, and more!

Sputum Chewies

What do you do with that wonderfully slimy, sticky blob you've coughed up? Don't waste it! Gather that flying phlegm and save it for your next party.

INGREDIENTS

3 envelopes unflavored gelatin
1¼ cups water, divided

1½ cups sugar
¼ teaspoon peppermint extract

Stove top

TOOLS YOU'LL NEED
• small mixing bowl • mixing spoon •
• medium saucepan with lid •
• whisk • pot holder • baking sheet • waxed paper

1 In a small mixing bowl, stir the gelatin into ½ cup water. Let mixture stand for five minutes to dissolve.

2 With an adult's help, bring the sugar and remaining ¾ cup water to a boil in a medium saucepan. Stir constantly with the whisk to prevent burning.

3 Add the dissolved gelatin mixture to the saucepan and reduce heat. Simmer, stirring constantly, for five minutes.

4 With a pot holder, have an adult help you remove the saucepan from the heat and place it on a heat-safe work surface. Add the peppermint extract to give the sputum a slight minty flavor. Blend thoroughly and allow ingredients to cool slightly. Then cover the pan and place it in the refrigerator for about 30 minutes to chill.

14

5 When the gelatin has partially thickened, use the whisk to lightly whip in natural-looking air bubbles into your sputum mixture. Line a baking sheet with waxed paper. Scoop generous tablespoonfuls of the gelatin onto the waxed paper. Leave about 2 inches between each sputum wad to allow for spreading. Set baking sheet in refrigerator for two hours or until firm.

6 Remove from refrigerator and let sputum stand at room temperature for three to four hours, turning over every hour with your clean hands, so both sides dry evenly. You can eat them now or cover unused sputum chewies tightly with plastic wrap and store them in the refrigerator. These are a great do-ahead party treat. You can make these up to one week in advance.

Makes: About 1 pound of hacked-up sputum (enough for 10 to 12 people)

Roach on a Coach

Don't freak out if there's a giant cockroach crawling on your food—he is *the food!*

INGREDIENTS

4 large carrots
8 oil-cured black olives
  with pits, such as Cento®

canned American cheese (such as
  Easy Cheese by Nabisco®)

TOOLS YOU'LL NEED
• nontoxic black felt-tip marker • 32 toothpicks
• vegetable peeler • utility knife • paring knife

1   With a black felt-tip marker, color 16 toothpicks black and set them aside for use later as your roach antennae.

2   With an adult's help, use a vegetable peeler to peel the carrots. Cut the ends off of each and discard. Starting at the widest portion of each carrot, use the utility knife to cut eight thin coin shapes, each about ¼-inch thick. These will be the car's wheels. Next, cut the remaining part of each carrot in half lengthwise. You will have eight carrot sticks, about 3 to 4 inches each, to be used as car bodies, and 32 round coin shapes to be used as wheels for your eight cars.

3   To create a car axle with wheels, poke one carrot round onto each end of an uncolored toothpick. Repeat with the remaining uncolored toothpicks and carrot rounds. Set them aside.

4 To create crawling roaches, have an adult help you use a paring knife to cut lengthwise about two-thirds down the center of an olive. Leave the remaining portion attached as the roach's head. Gently fan the olive meat away from the pit to form the roach's wings and body. Do not remove the pit. Repeat with the remaining olives.

5 Place one carrot-stick car body onto your work surface. Place one roach onto the middle of the car. To secure the roach in place, carefully but firmly poke two black-colored tooth-picks through the head portion into the car so that about half of each toothpick extends out as an antenna.

6 To assemble, place two sets of wheels onto your work surface. Lay a roach-covered car on top of each pair of axles, then carefully slide the carrot wheels in toward the carrot car body, so they hug up against the side of the car. To add larvae (baby roaches), place a generous squirt of American cheese underneath the roach, plus two more additional squirts behind it. They're ready to eat now. (This treat can be made a day in advance and kept tightly covered in the refrigerator.)

Serves: 8 roach relatives

FREAKY FACT:
Largest cockroach on record? It is 3.81 inches long—that's probably bigger than the palm of your hand! Forget the bug spray—you'd better start running if you cross paths with this one!

Cat Food Pâté on Toast

Who would have thought a can of ground-up intestines, fish eyes, and chicken heads and feet, covered with a coagulated, jiggling layer of slime, could taste so good? Here's a delicious variation on a feline favorite for those who "purrr-fur" copycat cat food to the real thing!

INGREDIENTS

6.75-ounce can deviled ham
8 slices processed American
  cheese

1 to 2 tablespoons Dijon mustard
1 envelope unflavored gelatin
crackers

Microwave/Stove top

TOOLS YOU'LL NEED

• microwave-safe mixing bowl • fork • plastic wrap •
• bowl • empty margarine tub, 1 cup size • cooking spray •
• rubber spatula • new, unused cat food bowl •

1 Empty the can of deviled ham into a microwave-safe mixing bowl, and use a fork to lightly fluff the ham. Break up the American cheese into bite-size pieces and fold them into the ham. Add the mustard and blend.

2 Cover bowl loosely with plastic wrap. Place the bowl into the microwave. Heat on high (100%) for about 45 seconds or until the cheese has melted. Ask an adult to help you remove it from microwave and set it aside to cool slightly. (This mixture may also be warmed in a small saucepan on low heat with an adult's help. Stir continuously until cheese is melted and all ingredients are thoroughly blended.)

3 With an adult's help, dissolve the gelatin in a bowl as directed on the package. To congeal the gelatin slightly, place it in the refrigerator for about 10 minutes.

4 Lightly coat the inside of the empty margarine tub with cooking spray. Use your spatula to scoop the deviled ham mixture into the tub. This will be your cat food can mold. Press down lightly with your spatula to remove air pockets, then invert the tub into your cat food bowl. If the cat food does not come out, gently but firmly tap the bottom of the plastic tub.

5 Pour the slightly congealed gelatin mixture over the top of your Cat Food Pâté. Then place the bowl in refrigerator to continue setting the gelatin (about 30 minutes). Serve immediately with crackers or cover tightly with plastic wrap. Can be stored up to five days in advance.

Serves: 8 fancy feasters

PUTRID PRESENTATION

Cats go wild for catnip! Use your kitchen scissors to snip fresh chives into inch-long pieces for catnip as a glorious garnish to your Cat Food Pâté. Arrange it decoratively along the edge of your serving platter.

Chilled Eyeballs

A treat just perfect for sucking on!

INGREDIENTS

⅔ cup water

1 small box Berry Blue–flavored
  Jell-O®

¼ cup shredded coconut

2 envelopes unflavored gelatin

2 cups milk

1 large package vanilla-flavored
  instant pudding and pie
  filling mix

24 black mini jelly beans

Stove top

TOOLS YOU'LL NEED

- paper towel • vegetable oil • 2 plastic egg-holding trays
  (from your refrigerator) • small saucepan • whisk
- medium mixing bowl • plastic wrap • warm, moist towel
  • small rubber spatula • serving platter

1 Moisten a section of paper towel with vegetable oil and rub it along the inside of each clean egg holder to prevent sticking. Be sure to coat each section thoroughly.

2 With an adult's help, bring ⅔ cup water to boil in a saucepan. Remove from heat and stir in the Jell-O using a whisk. Continue stirring for about two minutes or until completely dissolved. Spoon 1½ to 2 teaspoons dissolved Jell-O into each egg holder. Top each with a pinch of coconut (about ¼ teaspoon). Place the egg trays into the refrigerator to chill for exactly 40 minutes.

3 After about 30 minutes, begin preparing the "whites" of the eyes. Pour the unflavored gelatin into a liquid-measuring cup and dissolve gelatin according to the instructions on the package.

4   Pour the milk and instant pudding mix into a medium mixing bowl along with the dissolved gelatin. Whisk vigorously to blend ingredients completely. Set aside.

5   When the Jell-O has set for exactly 40 minutes, remove trays from the refrigerator and fill each egg holder to the rim with the pudding mixture. Refrigerate any excess pudding for snacking on later. The trays will be full, so carefully place them back in the refrigerator and chill for two to three hours. If you're not planning on serving these immediately, cover trays with plastic wrap and store, refrigerated, for up to one week.

6   An hour or two before you serve the eyeballs, carefully remove them from the egg trays. Rub a warm, moist towel along the bottom of each tray for a few minutes. Then carefully slide a small rubber spatula between each eyeball and the edge of its holder and pop the eyeball out. Repeat with the remaining eyeballs and arrange them on your serving platter.

7   Press one black jelly bean into the center of each blue iris. Refrigerate uneaten eyes.

Makes: 2 dozen eyesores

21

Potato Bug Bits

Begin an exciting career as an insect exterminator today! You can start with one of the biggest and ugliest beetles of all—the potato bug.

INGREDIENTS

6-ounce package barbecue-
  flavored potato chips

1 cup margarine

4 medium baking potatoes

32 pieces large puffed corn

12-ounce bag chow mein noodles

Microwave/Stove top and Oven

TOOLS YOU'LL NEED

- large reclosable plastic bag • rolling pin • small mixing bowl
- microwave-safe bowl • pot holders • paper towel • cutting board
- utility knife • 13- by 9- by 2-inch baking dish • fork • toothpick

1 Pour the potato chips into the reclosable bag, remove as much air as you can, and seal the bag. Place the bag on your work surface, and firmly roll the rolling pin over the chips to crush them thoroughly. Pour the crushed chips into a small mixing bowl and set aside.

2 Put the margarine into a microwave-safe bowl and heat on high (100%) for about 40 seconds or until the margarine has melted. Use pot holders and ask an adult to help you remove the bowl from the microwave. Set aside to cool slightly. (Margarine may also be melted in a small saucepan over low heat with an adult's help.)

3 With an adult's help, preheat oven to 350 degrees. Wash your potatoes and pat them lightly to dry with a paper towel. Place them on a cutting board and ask an adult to help you cut each potato lengthwise, with a utility knife, into eight equal, finger-shaped wedges.

4 Make an assembly line on your work surface consisting of potato wedges, bowl of melted butter, bowl of crushed chips, and 13- by 9- by 2-inch baking dish. To make a potato bug body, dip one wedge completely in the margarine. Place it into the bowl of chips and turn it over to coat both sides of potato wedge. Remove the potato bug from the bowl and lay it in the baking dish. Repeat with remaining ingredients. Arrange potato bugs in dish about ½ inch apart.

5 With an adult's help, place the dish in oven and bake for about 20 minutes. Then, using a fork and pot holders, carefully turn over each potato bug to brown the other side. Continue baking for 20 more minutes or until the potato bugs are soft in the center. Remove from oven and let potato bugs stand until they are cool enough for you to handle.

6 To make heads, poke two holes into each piece of puffed corn using a toothpick, then insert two chow mein noodles into each piece of puffed corn so that the noodles extend equally on each side.

7 Poke three chow mein noodles into the side of each potato bug body so that the noodles are equal on each side. This will form six legs per bug. Then carefully press one head into each potato bug so that the noodles stick out on one side and poke directly into the potato bug body on the other. Serve immediately. You can prepare potato bug heads up to one day ahead and store them in a tightly sealed container. Potato bug bodies can be made up to three hours in advance and stored, tightly covered, in the refrigerator. Just before serving, reheat them in the microwave on high (100%) for two to three minutes.

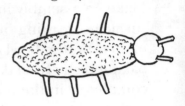

*Serves: 8 bugged buddies
(4 bugs apiece)*

PUTRID PRESENTATION

Assemble bugs on individual plates lying on their backs as if they've died in agony. Pour about 1 tablespoon barbecue sauce to serve as the bug's fresh and oozing blood.

CESSPOOL
OF *SWEETS*

Dustpan
Pudding
(page 28)

Toenail
Trimmings
(page 32)

**Bloody
Broken Glass**
(page 35)

Outhouse Delight

Here's one nasty pile of dessert tasty enough to feed the whole gang!

INGREDIENTS

6 ounces white chocolate chips

¼ cup light corn syrup

5.1-ounce package chocolate-flavored instant pudding and pie filling mix

1 quart milk (not 3 cups as directed on pudding box), well chilled

16-ounce can ready-made German chocolate cake frosting

12 dark chocolate cookies, broken into chunks

Stove top

TOOLS YOU'LL NEED

• double boiler • rubber spatula • small mixing bowl • plastic wrap • waxed paper • rolling pin • ruler • utility knife • large mixing bowl • whisk • ladle • soup bowls

1 The toilet tissue dough requires several hours to fully set, so you may wish to make this at least one day in advance. Fill the lower portion of your double boiler with water. With an adult's help, heat the water over medium heat. In the upper portion of the boiler, add the white chocolate chips and corn syrup.

2 Stir constantly with a rubber spatula until mixture is smooth. Remove from heat and carefully pour the chocolate mixture into a small mixing bowl. Set it aside to cool to room temperature. Cover with plastic wrap *directly touching* your chocolate toilet tissue dough, and let it stand until the mixture becomes shiny and doughy.

3 After the dough has set, place it onto your work surface between two sheets of waxed paper, and press the dough into a disc. Use a rolling pin to flatten the dough to an ⅛-inch thickness. Then pull off the top layer of waxed paper to prevent it from sticking to the tissue mixture.

4 Using your ruler and utility knife, have an adult help you cut the dough into eight 2-inch squares of toilet tissue. Turn dough over on your work surface and remove the lower layer of waxed paper. With clean, dry hands, gently crumple the individual squares to create a realistic-looking toilet tissue wad. Set them aside, tightly covered with plastic wrap, at room temperature.

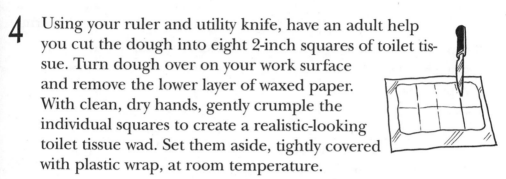

5 Pour the instant chocolate pudding mix and the milk into a large mixing bowl, and whisk vigorously for two minutes to blend ingredients thoroughly. Scoop the German chocolate frosting into the pudding mixture by rounded teaspoonfuls. Pour in the crushed cookies and fold together lightly with the spatula to create a wonderfully lumpy outhouse dump mixture.

6 Ladle dump mixture into soup bowls. Place one ball of crumpled toilet paper in the center of each bowl and serve immediately. You can prepare the dough (steps 1 and 2 only) up to three days in advance and store it, covered, at room temperature. Then roll it out and crumple it a few hours before serving. Outhouse Delight is most natural looking and runny when prepared just before serving. Store leftovers in the refrigerator.

Makes: 8 bowls of soupy poopies

Dustpan Pudding

If people have ever told you not to eat off the floor, they have no idea what they're missing. This pile of dirt is downright delicious!

INGREDIENTS

¾ cup any type light-colored crunchy sugar cookie*

¾ cup graham crackers*

1 cup any type dark chocolate crunchy cookie*

2 packages (3.5 to 4 ounces each) vanilla-flavored instant pudding and pie filling mix

4 cups milk

8-ounce container nondairy whipped topping

1 box (10½ ounces) miniature chocolate chip cookies

16 snips of shoelace licorice (of varied lengths from 1 to 3 inches), any color

8 to 10 gold-foil-wrapped coins, foils removed

candy rocks (realistic candy rocks, available at candy shops and many supermarkets)

* To measure cookies properly, crush them slightly before filling the measuring cup.

TOOLS YOU'LL NEED

- food processor, fitted with metal chopping blade
- large mixing bowl • mixing spoon • whisk • rubber spatula
- 2½-quart serving bowl • plastic wrap

1 Ask an adult to help you pour the crushed sugar cookies, graham crackers, and dark chocolate cookies into a food processor. Thoroughly blend until crumbs are the consistency of granulated sugar. Set aside. (If you do not have a food processor, place all three cookie types into a reclosable plastic bag, remove excess air, and seal. Crush thoroughly with a rolling pin.)

2 In a large mixing bowl, prepare both pudding mixes with milk according to package directions. Use a whisk to mix thoroughly.

3 With a rubber spatula, fold in the whipped topping and chocolate chip cookies.

4 To assemble, spoon half of the pudding mixture into a serving bowl. Then sprinkle with half of the cookie dust. Repeat with a second layer of each. Cover with plastic wrap and refrigerate for at least four hours. This portion can be prepared up to one day in advance. Just before serving your dust pile, decorate with things you've "swept off the floor": licorice snips as thread, chocolate coins, and candy rocks. Be sure guests get at least one rock and a piece of thread on their dust pile.

Serves: 16 dust bunnies

PUTRID PRESENTATION

Ask Mom to buy you a new dustpan to use *only* when you're serving this delicious dessert. Serve guests their pudding in individual bowls. Then, using a clean pastry brush, dust off the decorative thread, rocks, and coins into each guest's bowl. What a great way to dispose of your dirt!

Feces Pieces

These bite-sized bits of thick, pasty poops look like they took loads of effort to push out—but you can put these together in no time!

INGREDIENTS

¾ cup chunky peanut butter

¼ cup unsweetened cocoa

¼ cup butter or margarine, softened

1 cup flaked coconut

½ cup finely chopped walnuts

½ cup corn, frozen, thawed, and drained

2 to 2½ cups confectioners' sugar, divided

TOOLS YOU'LL NEED

• baking sheet • waxed paper • large mixing bowl
• electric mixer • cutting board or marble pastry board
• plastic wrap

1 Line a baking sheet with waxed paper and set aside. Clear a spot in the refrigerator big enough to fit the baking sheet.

2 Place the peanut butter, unsweetened cocoa, and butter or margarine into a mixing bowl. Ask an adult to help you use an electric mixer to mix thoroughly until creamed.

3 Add in the coconut, walnuts, corn, and 1 cup confectioners' sugar. Mix on lowest speed until blended well.

4 Sprinkle some of the remaining sugar onto your cutting board or marble pastry board. Place the peanut butter mixture onto the board and knead in 1 cup confectioners' sugar with your clean, dry hands. Continue kneading until it's thoroughly blended. The mixture should hold its shape

easily when formed. If it is not firm enough, add additional powdered sugar a tablespoon at a time.

5 To shape feces, scoop one rounded tablespoonful into your hands and roll into a poop shape. Place on the paper-lined baking sheet. Repeat with remaining dough. Each poop is unique, so shape each one differently.

6 Cover Feces Pieces with plastic wrap and place in the refrigerator for one hour to harden them. These satisfying bowel movements can be made up to one week in advance and stored in the refrigerator, covered tightly.

Makes: 2 dozen little stinkers

FREAKY FACT:

Though nobody on record has ever died from constipation, there have been some mighty long cases of bathroom absenteeism—many over one year! That could add up to anywhere from 60 to 100 pounds of excess poop—not to mention a great deal of discomfort!

Toenail Trimmings

A delectable treat for all the nail-biters on your guest list. Toenail trimmings are a truly habit-forming delicacy!

INGREDIENTS

1½ cups confectioners' sugar
1 cup butter, softened
1 egg
1½ teaspoons vanilla extract
2¾ cups all-purpose flour, divided
1 teaspoon baking soda
1 teaspoon cream of tartar

For nail polish:
2 cups confectioners' sugar
¼ cup light corn syrup
2 tablespoons water
red and orange food coloring
blue food coloring (optional)

Oven

TOOLS YOU'LL NEED

• large mixing bowl • electric mixer • plastic wrap • rolling pin
• ruler • flat saucer • 3 different-sized round cookie cutters or
round plastic-container lids • baking sheet, greased • pot holders
• flat metal spatula • wire rack • medium mixing bowl • whisk
• 3 small mixing bowls • small rubber spatula

1 Combine confectioners' sugar, butter, egg, vanilla, 2¼ cups flour, baking soda, and cream of tartar into a large mixing bowl. Ask an adult to help you use the electric mixer to blend ingredients first on low speed, then on medium, until thoroughly blended. Remove dough from mixing bowl and cover tightly in plastic wrap. Chill dough in the refrigerator for two to three hours or overnight.

2 When the dough has chilled, ask an adult to help you pre-heat the oven to 375 degrees. With some of the remaining flour, lightly flour your work surface and rolling pin. Remove one-third of the dough from the refrigerator and roll it to ¼-inch thickness.

3 Place about ¼ cup of the remaining flour into a flat saucer to be used for flouring toenail cookie cutters. To cut toenails, dip each cookie cutter or plastic lid into the flour to coat it lightly. Starting at the edge of the dough, cut out thin crescent shapes. Lay the toenails onto a greased baking sheet. Each toenail should be about ¾ inch to 1 inch wide at the center of the toenail. Length of clippings will vary with the size of cookie cutter. Repeat with remaining dough. Note: Baking time will be less for small toenails and more for large ones, so bake sizes separately.

4 Use pot holders and ask an adult to help you place the greased baking sheet into the oven. Bake for five to seven minutes or until lightly browned. Have an adult help you remove the toenails from the oven and let them set for a minute. Use a flat metal spatula to transfer them to a wire rack to cool completely.

5 To prepare nail polish, place the confectioners' sugar, corn syrup, and water into a medium mixing bowl. Blend thoroughly with your whisk until all sugar lumps are dissolved. Divide mixture evenly into three small mixing bowls. Add a few drops of red food coloring to one bowl to create red nail polish and a few drops of orange food coloring to another bowl to create orange nail polish. Leave the remaining bowl uncolored for a white polish, or add a few drops of blue to this last bowl for a hot new high-fashion shade.

6 While they are still on the rack, polish the nail clippings using a small rubber spatula.

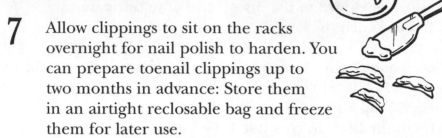

7 Allow clippings to sit on the racks overnight for nail polish to harden. You can prepare toenail clippings up to two months in advance: Store them in an airtight reclosable bag and freeze them for later use.

Makes: About 6 dozen toenail trimming treats

FREAKY FACT:

Fingernails grow at a rate of about 0.02 inches a week—that's about four times faster than toenails. So, cherish these crunchy toenails— they've taken a long time to prepare!

Bloody Broken Glass

This dessert is truly a cut above the rest!

INGREDIENTS

1 cup light corn syrup

1 cup water

2 cups sugar

½ teaspoon clear-colored candy
flavoring oil (such as lemon or
peppermint)

6 ounces red confectionery
coating

| Stove top |

TOOLS YOU'LL NEED

• nonstick baking sheet with a raised edge, or baking sheet,
lightly greased • large, heavy saucepan with lid • wooden spoon
• pot holders • candy thermometer • waxed paper
• double boiler • whisk

1 Place the baking sheet in the refrigerator to chill.

2 Pour the corn syrup, water, and sugar into a heavy saucepan.
Ask an adult to help you heat the mixture over medium-
high heat. Use a wooden spoon to stir constantly until sugar
dissolves.

3 Bring the mixture to a boil. Cover the pan and continue
boiling for about three minutes so steam can melt any sugar
crystals that have built up on the sides of the saucepan.

4 Remove the lid using pot holders. Be sure to have an adult
help you. Place the candy thermometer into the sugar
mixture, and rest it on or clip it to the side of the saucepan.
Continue to cook the mixture, uncovered, without stirring,

over high heat until thermometer reads 310 degrees or "hard crack" stage.

5 Remove pan from heat and place it on a pot holder on your work surface. Allow it to cool to 160 degrees. Then stir in the candy flavoring oil with the wooden spoon.

6 Remove the baking sheet from the refrigerator and place it on your work surface. With your hands protected by pot holders, hold the chilled baking sheet and have an adult pour the candy mixture onto the baking sheet. Quickly tip the baking sheet back and forth to spread the hot sugar mixture as evenly and thinly as possible to create clear "glass." (Do not attempt to scrape the cooking pan to remove excess sugar mixture. Instead, place the pan under hot water to dissolve the sugar and wash the pan out.) Return baking sheet to the refrigerator.

7 When the candy glass has hardened, lay waxed paper down on your work surface. Crack the candy into pieces of all shapes and sizes and set them on the waxed paper.

8 Fill the lower portion of a double boiler half full with water. With an adult's help, place the double boiler on the stove and turn burner on medium heat. When the water begins to simmer, pour the confectionery coating into the upper portion. Stir occasionally with a whisk while coating melts.

9 With an adult's help, turn heat to lowest possible setting to prevent coating from thickening. Place a length of waxed paper on a suitable work surface close to the double boiler.

10 Quickly dip the tips of a piece of broken glass into the melted "blood" and hold it upright so that drips form as the coating hardens. Place it on the waxed paper to cool and set. Repeat with the remaining pieces of glass. You can prepare Bloody Broken Glass up to two weeks in advance: Put waxed paper between each layer of glass and store the glass in a tightly sealed container lined with waxed paper.

Makes: About 1¼ pounds shattered shards

PUTRID PRESENTATION

Add variety to your bloody accident by coloring the glass in popular bottle colors, such as brown or green. Simply add a few drops of green food coloring, or equal parts red and green to make a classic beer-bottle brown.

Cryonic Creeps

*You'll just die over these chilly bodies! They're frozen for science—
and for you and your friends to enjoy anytime.*

INGREDIENTS

4 eggs

1¼ cups sugar

⅛ teaspoon salt

⅓ cup cornstarch

4 cups milk

14-ounce can sweetened
condensed milk

2 tablespoons vanilla extract

16 small candy eyes or any small,
round candies

1 cup popped corn

Stove top

TOOLS YOU'LL NEED

• medium mixing bowl • whisk • large, heavy saucepan
• wooden spoon • pot holders • can opener • plastic wrap
• 8 gingerbread man molds (available at craft and baking
supply stores) • serving plates

1 Beat the eggs in a medium mixing bowl with a whisk. Gradually add the sugar, salt, and cornstarch. Continue beating until thoroughly blended. Set aside.

2 Pour the milk into a large, heavy saucepan. Ask an adult to help you bring the milk to a boil, stirring constantly with a wooden spoon to prevent it from burning.

3 Using pot holders, have an adult pour about ¼ cup hot milk into the egg mixture. Mix lightly with your whisk, then pour the mixture into the saucepan. This process prevents the egg mixture from clumping.

4 Continue cooking the mixture, stirring constantly with the wooden spoon for six to eight minutes or until mixture thickens and coats the spoon. Open the sweetened condensed milk with a can opener. Gradually stir in the canned milk and vanilla and mix well. Remove the saucepan from your stove top and place on a heat-safe work surface.

5 Allow the custard mixture to cool, then cover the saucepan with plastic wrap and place it in the refrigerator for three to four hours.

6 Meanwhile, line your gingerbread man molds with plastic wrap, pressing the plastic wrap into the mold's crevices. Be sure to leave enough plastic hanging over the sides so that you can grab on to it when you're ready to unmold the men. Fill each mold about three-quarters full with custard mixture. Cover each mold with plastic wrap and place it in the freezer for three to four hours or overnight to harden.

7 To serve, let Cryonic Creeps stand at room temperature for about five minutes. Then unmold each treat onto individual serving plates and carefully peel away its plastic wrap. Decorate each person with two individual candy eyes and popped corn for bushy hair. Serve immediately. You can freeze these dead guys up to one week in advance and unmold as directed. Decorate just before serving.

Makes: 8 cool cadavers

Amputated Tongues

Tongues will be a waggin' over these easy-to-make delectable desserts!

INGREDIENTS

1 pound pink confectionery coating   white nonpareils
16-ounce package Nutter Butter®
  peanut butter cookies

Stove top

TOOLS YOU'LL NEED
• double boiler • pot holders • whisk
• waxed paper • tongs • small rubber spatula

1 Fill the lower portion of a double boiler halfway with water. With an adult's help, place the double boiler on the stove and turn burner on medium heat. When the water begins to simmer, pour the confectionery coating into the upper portion. Stir occasionally with a whisk while coating melts.

2 With an adult's help, turn heat to lowest possible setting to prevent coating from thickening. Place a length of waxed paper on a suitable work surface close to the double boiler.

3 To assemble tongues, ask an adult to hold the pan with pot holders while you dip the cookies. Using tongs, pick up one cookie and completely dip it into the melted pink coating. Lift it up, allowing excess coating to drip off, and place it onto the waxed paper. Immediately sprinkle white nonpareils lightly over the tongue to make taste buds. Repeat with the remaining cookies.

4 To cover the uncoated areas on the tongues left by the tongs, dip a small rubber spatula into the melted pink coating and spread it over the uncovered portion. Allow the cookies to cool completely. Store the tongues, covered, at room temperature for up to three days, or frozen, in a tightly sealed container, for up to two months.

Makes: About 3 dozen tasty tongues

PUTRID PRESENTATION

Hairy tongue is a strange but real malady in which a person's tongue actually appears to grow hair! Why not create an entire batch of wonderfully hairy tongues to tempt the whole gang? Add black food coloring to ½ cup shredded coconut. Then, instead of the white nonpareils, sprinkle the black coconut over the tops of the freshly dipped tongues.

Hairballs

Enjoy this hairy delicacy when your cat is shedding its fur.
They certainly taste better than the real thing!

INGREDIENTS

1 roll ready-made chocolate cookie dough (with nuts or chips, optional)

7-ounce bag sweetened shredded coconut

black, orange, or brown food coloring (the color of your kitty's fur)

16-ounce can ready-to-spread chocolate frosting

Oven

TOOLS YOU'LL NEED

- butter knife • baking sheet, lightly greased
- pot holders • metal spatula • wire racks
- small mixing bowl • fork • small rubber spatula

1 With a butter knife, cut the dough log into 12 even slices. (Each slice should equal about 2 generous tablespoons.)

2 To shape hairballs, roll a section of dough between your clean, dry hands into a tube shape about ½ inch by 2 inches. Repeat with remaining dough. Arrange cookies about 2 inches apart on lightly greased baking sheet.

3 With an adult's help, preheat oven to 350 degrees. Place baking sheet in freezer and chill for about 15 minutes or until dough is firm.

4 Ask an adult to help you remove the hairballs from the freezer and place them in the oven. Bake about 15 minutes or until set. Using pot holders, have an adult help you remove them from the oven.

5 With an adult's help, use a metal spatula to remove the cookies from baking sheet and place them on wire racks to cool. Pour the shredded coconut into a small mixing bowl and add food coloring of your choice, drop by drop, until you've matched your kitty's coat color. Mix thoroughly with a fork to distribute the food coloring.

6 When cookies have cooled completely, spread the tops and sides of each cookie with chocolate frosting using a rubber spatula. Then roll each hairball in the coconut, pressing with your hands to help the coconut stick to the hairball. Allow hairballs to air dry for two to three hours or overnight before serving. After drying, hairballs can be served immediately or frozen for up to two months in a tightly sealed container. Do not overlap hairballs when storing, and be sure to put waxed paper between layers.

Makes: 12 clumps of kitty coat

FREAKY FACT:

The largest recorded domestic cat was a male tabby named Himmy, owned by Thomas Vyse of Redlynch, Queensland, Australia. Himmy weighed in at a whopping 46 pounds, 15¼ ounces and had a massive 33-inch waistline! One can only wonder . . . do big cats make big hairballs?

Doggie-Drop Cookies

Move over, Rover. These doggie leftovers are worth a second bite!

INGREDIENTS

1½ cups semi-sweet
   chocolate chips
½ cup chunky peanut butter

2 tablespoons butter or
   margarine
36 large marshmallows

Microwave/Stove top

TOOLS YOU'LL NEED
- baking sheet • waxed paper
- large microwave-safe bowl • plastic wrap
- pot holders • rubber spatula
- metal spatula • serving plates

1 Clear a space in the refrigerator large enough for a baking sheet. Line the baking sheet with waxed paper and set aside.

2 Pour the semi-sweet chocolate chips, peanut butter, and butter or margarine into a large microwave-safe bowl. Cover lightly with plastic wrap. With an adult's help, microwave on high (100%) for about one and a half minutes. Use pot holders to remove bowl from microwave. Stir well with a rubber spatula. Cover and return to the microwave. Cook on high for approximately one and a half minutes longer and stir again. Repeat until chocolate chips are smooth and melted. (This step may also be done with an adult's help using a double boiler on the stove.)

3 Allow the chocolate mixture to cool slightly, about two to three minutes. Fold in the marshmallows and stir with the rubber spatula to coat completely with the chocolate mixture.

4 When the chocolate mixture has cooled enough for you to handle with your clean, dry hands, remove marshmallows from chocolate mixture and arrange them in sets of three onto your baking sheet. Keeping marshmallows close together, form random doggie-poop shapes.

5 Drizzle the remaining chocolate mixture evenly over each doggie dropping. Note: If excess chocolate mixture spreads too far from the poop, use the rubber spatula to push it back into shape.

6 Chill for about an hour (or until firm) in the refrigerator. Store doggie droppings, covered, in the refrigerator for up to three days. These can be made ahead and frozen, tightly covered, for up to two months. Just before serving, carefully lift the droppings from the lined baking sheet using a metal spatula and transfer them to individual serving plates. Serve with forks so guests can scoop their plates clean plop by plop.

Makes: 12 doggie dinners

SNIFF!!
SNIFF!!

PUTRID PRESENTATION

Large marshmallows will produce German shepherd–sized doggie dung, but you can serve up a batch of poodle-sized poops, too, by using mini marshmallows instead. You'll need about 3 cups mini marshmallows.

Kitty Litter Clumps

They're stinkin' good!

INGREDIENTS

4 medium-sized bananas

3 cups peanuts or walnuts

1 cup chunky peanut butter

6 ounces dark chocolate
confectionery coating

blue jimmie sprinkles or Betty
Crocker® Party Sugar

Microwave/Stove top

TOOLS YOU'LL NEED

- utility knife • food processor fitted with metal chopping blade
- 13- by 9- by 2-inch baking dish • large microwave-safe bowl
- plastic wrap • pot holders • rubber spatula • tongs

1 With an adult's help, use a utility knife to
cut each banana in half widthwise, then
lengthwise. You will have 16 finger-shaped
banana wedges. Set them aside.

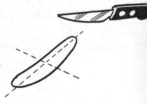

2 With an adult's help, pour the peanuts or walnuts into the
food processor. Chop nuts into kitty litter–sized chunks
similar to rough sand. Spread the nuts into a 13- by 9- by 2-
inch baking dish and set aside.

3 Place the chunky peanut butter and dark chocolate confectionery coating into a microwave-safe bowl. Cover lightly with
plastic wrap. With an adult's help, microwave on high (100%)
for about one minute. Use pot holders to remove bowl from
microwave. Stir well with a rubber spatula. Cover and return to
microwave. Cook on high for approximately one more minute
and stir again. Repeat until chocolate chunks are completely

melted. Use pot holders to place the bowl on your work surface. (The peanut butter and chocolate may also be melted with an adult's help using a double boiler.)

4 To create kitty dumps, begin completely coating the banana chunks by dipping them into the melted chocolate mixture with tongs. You'll want to do this step quickly. Lay them on the bed of chopped nuts and roll them with tongs so that all sides are coated. Then liberally sprinkle all sides with blue jimmies or Betty Crocker® Party Sugar to create the flecks of colored deodorizing crystals that keep the stench away—almost!

5 Move the kitty litter dumps off to one side while you continue coating the remaining bananas. Leave excess jimmies or crystals mixed in with the nuts as you continue coating bananas. Before serving, bury some of the cat poops in the remaining nuts, as any polite cat would, and lightly sprinkle additional jimmies or crystals over the entire tray. Cover lightly and store in the refrigerator. Kitty Litter Clumps can be made two to three hours in advance, or covered tightly and frozen up to two weeks in advance. If you freeze them, move the tray to the refrigerator 20 minutes before serving. Do not refreeze.

Makes: 16 fancy feline feces

MORBID
MUNCHIES

Brain Cell
Salad
(page 62)

Handwiches
(page 64)

Bad Breath
Biscuits
(page 68)

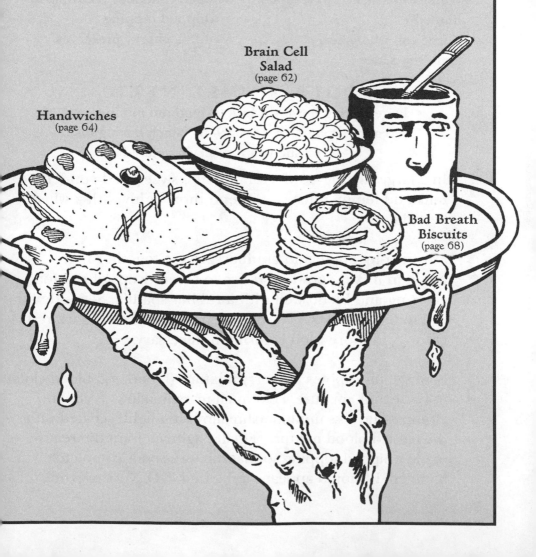

Cellulite Salad

Straight from your plastic surgeon's "waist" basket, this fatty, lumpy, clumpy salad makes a delicious side dish!

INGREDIENTS

14-ounce can sweetened condensed milk

¼ cup lemon juice

20-ounce can crushed pineapple, drained

16-ounce can whole-berry cranberry sauce

red food coloring

2 cups mini marshmallows

2 cups large marshmallows

8-ounce container ready-made whipped topping

½ cup raspberry preserves

TOOLS YOU'LL NEED

• large mixing bowl • whisk • medium mixing bowl
• rubber spatula • 13- by 9- by 2-inch baking dish
• plastic wrap • serving plates

1 In a large mixing bowl, combine the sweetened condensed milk and lemon juice, and blend thoroughly with a whisk. Set aside.

2 Stir the pineapple and cranberry sauce together in a medium mixing bowl. Add five to seven drops of red food coloring and blend well with a rubber spatula. Set aside for five to ten minutes or until pineapple takes on a dark red color. Add more food coloring if necessary.

3 Fold the pineapple-cranberry mixture (blood and blood clots) into the milk mixture. Fold in all marshmallows (cellulite clumps) and toss until marshmallows are lightly coated with the clotted blood mixture. Finally, lightly fold in the ready-made whipped topping so that mixture is not completely blended. It should appear marbleized. DO NOT overmix.

50

4 Spoon the cellulite mixture into a 13- by 9- by 2-inch baking dish. Use a tablespoon to scoop up dollops of raspberry preserves (clots of thickened blood). Hold each scoop about 12 inches above the cellulite salad, and allow it to drop and splatter onto the salad.

5 Cover tightly with plastic wrap and freeze until firm, about four hours or overnight. Allow cellulite to sit at room temperature for about 10 minutes before scooping it onto individual serving plates. May be prepared up to one week in advance and stored, tightly covered, in the freezer.

Serves: 12 to 16 blubber lovers

PUTRID PRESENTATION

Did that sloppy plastic surgeon suck up some veins along with the cellulite? Fold several pieces of red or black shoelace licorice into the salad. Leave some veins buried in the cellulite and hang other pieces over the sides like wiggling arteries.

Taxidermist's Leftovers

Taxidermy, the art of stuffing dead animals for display, is a job with added benefits! Entrails, bones, and unidentifiable body parts blend together for this light and yummy side dish. It's especially delicious when you're feeling a little "stuffed."

INGREDIENTS

4 cups fresh or fresh frozen
  cranberries
¼ cup water
8 baking apples

1 pear
2 small bananas
1 cup sugar

Stove top

TOOLS YOU'LL NEED

- large, heavy saucepan with lid • vegetable peeler and corer
- paring knife • sieve • fork • wooden spoon
- large serving bowl • plastic wrap

1 Place the cranberries and water into a heavy saucepan. With an adult's help, place the saucepan over burner and simmer for 20 to 25 minutes or until tender. Set aside to cool to room temperature.

2 Have an adult help you peel the apples and pear with the vegetable peeler. With the paring knife, cut the pear in half lengthwise and remove the seeds. Cut four of the peeled apples into eight finger-shaped wedges and remove the seeds. Cut the fifth apple in half widthwise and the sixth apple in half lengthwise.

Remove seeds. Core the remaining two apples, which means remove the seeds and leave the apples whole. Peel the bananas and cut one in half widthwise, and the other one in half lengthwise, then widthwise. Now your taxidermy pieces are in a wide variety of unidentifiable body shapes. Set these body parts aside.

3 When the cranberries have cooled, press them with your clean hands through a sieve to extract the juice. Collect the juice in the saucepan. Discard skins and pulp.

4 Add all the apples and pear pieces to the cranberry juice. With an adult's help, place the saucepan over burner and simmer, covered, for about 30 minutes. Add the bananas and continue simmering for 10 to 15 minutes or until the whole apples are tender. To test, stick a fork into an apple— it should glide in easily. Add the sugar and gently stir with a wooden spoon to coat fruit in the sauce. The bananas will break apart slightly and give the appearance of membrane and cartilage. Simmer for five more minutes, stirring occasionally. Transfer to a large serving bowl and chill, tightly covered with plastic wrap, in refrigerator until you're ready to serve. Taxidermist's Leftovers can be made up to two days in advance.

Serves: 8 to 10 boneless buddies

PUTRID PRESENTATION

Get guests into a "wild" mood! Create an animal-pelt placemat for each guest out of squares of fake fur (available at fabric supply stores).

Rotten Eggs

If you're scrambling for a last-minute side dish, whip up some of these rotten-egg look-alikes. These fruit-and-custard egg impostors appear to be massively moldy sunny-side-up eggs.

INGREDIENTS

1 cup ready-made whipped
  topping
green food coloring
5.1-ounce package instant vanilla-
  flavored pudding and pie
  filling mix

3½ cups cold milk
16-ounce can peach halves,
  drained

TOOLS YOU'LL NEED

• small mixing bowl • whisk • large mixing bowl • dessert plates

1   Place the ready-made whipped topping into a small mixing bowl. Add two or three drops of green food coloring and blend well with a whisk to create a light green shade of mold. Be careful not to overstir. Set aside.

2   Pour the instant vanilla pudding mix and milk into a large mixing bowl. (Note: This is slightly more milk than suggested in the directions on the pudding box, but these rotten eggs are supposed to be a bit runny and undercooked!) To blend ingredients, whisk for about two minutes, then pour at once into individual dessert plates, dividing evenly. This will be the white portion of the rotten eggs.

3   Arrange one peach half in the center of each egg white. To add rotten mold to your sunny-side-up eggs, scoop out one rounded teaspoonful of the green whipped-topping mixture.

Hold it high above one of the eggs and allow it to drop and splatter on the egg. Repeat one or two more times.

4 Splatter the rest of the dessert plates with the greenish mixture. Place the plates in the refrigerator for about 15 minutes before serving. You can prepare the mold and rotten-egg whites in advance. Cover tightly with plastic wrap and store in the refrigerator up to a day ahead. Then, before serving, do steps 3 and 4.

Serves: 6 egg-centric friends

PUTRID PRESENTATION

Toss a small handful of "cracked eggshells" (hardened mini marshmallows) in for added texture!

Maggot Man

This larvae-infested freak is sure to turn some heads at your next potluck!

INGREDIENTS

2 tablespoons butter or
margarine
½ cup chopped onion
2 cups uncooked long-grain
white rice
4 cups chicken or vegetable broth
1 tablespoon dried parsley flakes
2 teaspoons dried basil
1 teaspoon poultry seasoning
½ teaspoon salt
½ teaspoon pepper
¾ cup grated Jack cheese

For decorating:
2 cauliflower florets*
1 circular slice green bell pepper,
cut in half*
1 circular slice from a red bell
pepper end (the bumpy bottom), cut in half*
1 baby carrot
ice cubes
3 leaves fresh kale
2 peas
1 cherry tomato
2 slices black olive

* Save remaining portions of vegetables for your next meal, or chop them
up and stir-fry with a few tablespoons oil as a separate side dish.

Stove top

TOOLS YOU'LL NEED

• large, covered saucepan • wooden spoon • 6-cup capacity round
serving bowl • plastic wrap • medium saucepan
• colander • pot holders • round serving platter, about 2 inches
larger around than your serving bowl

1 To prepare the maggot filling, place the butter or margarine
and onion in a large saucepan. With an adult's help, place
saucepan on a burner and melt butter over medium heat.
Cook onion till soft. Use a wooden spoon to stir in the rice,

broth, parsley, basil, poultry seasoning, salt, and pepper. Bring mixture to a boil. Cover saucepan and reduce heat to low. Simmer 20 to 25 minutes or until rice is tender.

2 While the rice is simmering, line a round serving bowl with plastic wrap. Set aside.

3 Fill a medium saucepan halfway with water. With an adult's help, bring water to a boil over high heat. Add the cauliflower, green and red bell peppers, and carrot. Boil for three minutes to soften the vegetables. Get an adult to help you pour the boiling water and vegetables into a colander to drain. (Be sure to use pot holders.) Refill the saucepan with water and the ice cubes. Return vegetables to saucepan to stop the cooking process. Set aside.

4 When the rice mixture is done, remove the large saucepan from heat with an adult's help, and stir in the cheese using the wooden spoon. Spoon mixture into the serving bowl lined with plastic wrap. Cover the top with more plastic wrap and press down firmly to mold rice mixture into the shape of the bowl—Maggot Man's head. Remove the top layer of plastic wrap and let stand for 10 minutes.

5 To assemble Maggot Man's head, place the kale leaves close together around the rim of the serv-ing platter. The leaves will be his wild and bushy hairdo. With an adult's help, invert the bowl onto the platter over the kale. Gently pat the bottom of bowl to loosen the rice. Remove bowl, leaving the plastic wrap over the maggot filling. With your hands over the plastic wrap, shape the filling into an oval by gently but firmly pressing in on the sides. Remove plastic wrap and discard.

6 Create his facial features using the cooked vegetables as follows:
- eyes: cauliflower florets, with a pea on top of each
- nose: cherry tomato
- eyebrows: break each olive slice and pull it into a semi-straight line
- ears: a green bell pepper slice on each side
- mouth: carrot placed vertically for an undulating uvula, and red bell pepper slices for upper and lower lips

Note: Maggot filling can be made up to three days ahead of time. Follow steps 1 through 4 and refrigerate, tightly covered, until you're ready to serve. At that time, microwave on high (100%) for three to four minutes. Decorate as directed in steps 5 and 6 and serve.

Serves: 10 to 12 maggot munchers

PUTRID PRESENTATION

Set the mood for all your fly larvae– loving buddies and pop the cult classic *The Fly* into the VCR after dinner.

Bowel Bundles

*No human waste here! Every bowl will be a tidy one
when you're serving this entrail treat.*

INGREDIENTS

4 cups all-purpose flour, divided,
  plus extra for kneading

2 packages instant yeast

½ teaspoon salt

½ cup very warm (not boiling)
  water

2 tablespoons olive oil

6 foot-long hot dogs

Oven

TOOLS YOU'LL NEED
- **large mixing bowl** • **whisk** • **dish towel**
- **utility knife** • **rolling pin** • **ruler**
- **baking sheet, greased and floured** • **pot holders**

1 In a large mixing bowl, combine 2 cups flour with the yeast and salt. Use a whisk to gently stir ingredients. Pour the very warm water and olive oil into the dry ingredients and continue stirring until a sticky batter is formed.

2 Slowly add the remaining flour and mix together with your clean, dry hands until it forms a moist (but not sticky) ball of dough.

3 Sprinkle flour lightly over your work surface and place the dough in the center. Using the palms of your hands, knead the dough for about six minutes or until dough is smooth. Do not overknead, as dough will become chewy. Return dough to the large mixing bowl and cover it with a dry dish towel. Place bowl in a warm, dry place for 10 minutes.

4 While you're waiting, ask an adult to help you preheat the oven to 475 degrees. Then, using your utility knife, cut slices into the hot dogs. The slices should go about three-fourths of the way into each hot dog widthwise, about 1 inch apart. This will allow the hot dog "bowels" to be easily bent and twisted after covering them in dough. Be careful not to cut all the way through the hot dogs. Set them aside.

5 Divide the dough into two balls and set one aside. Place the other ball of dough on a lightly floured surface and gently pat it flat with your hands. Then rub flour on a rolling pin and roll it back and forth over the dough. Shape it into a 9- by 12-inch rectangle.

6 Ask an adult to help you cut the dough into three 3- by 12-inch pieces. To assemble twisted bowels, lay one hot dog lengthwise on one 12-inch side of dough and carefully wrap the dough around the hot dog. Press the seam together with your fingers. Slowly bend and curl the bowel into an intestinal shape, then place it on your greased and floured baking sheet. Repeat with the two remaining dough pieces and hot dogs, making each bowel look different.

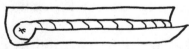

Note: If you need additional dough to cover bowels, this recipe can be doubled.

7 Repeat steps 5 and 6 with the remaining ball of dough and hot dogs. Use pot holders and, with an adult to help you, place the baking sheet into the oven for 10 to 15 minutes or until bowels turn golden and hot dogs are warmed through. Have an adult help you remove bowels from oven and allow them to cool slightly before serving. Bowels can also be made a few hours in advance and then served at room temperature.

Makes: 6 bundles of bowels

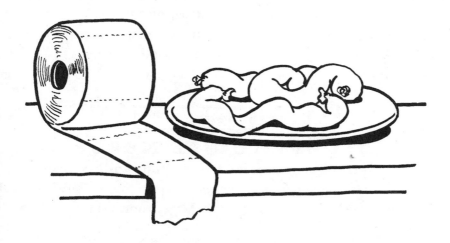

Brain Cell Salad

Even the brain-dead can mastermind this simple salad!

INGREDIENTS

4 eggs

ice cubes

1 medium onion

4 stalks celery

16-ounce package large
  elbow macaroni

1 cup mayonnaise

¼ cup sweet pickle relish

1 tablespoon white-wine vinegar

1 tablespoon mustard

¾ teaspoon salt

¼ teaspoon celery seed

black food coloring

Stove top

TOOLS YOU'LL NEED

• small saucepan • pot holders • utility knife • grater •
• large, heavy saucepan • colander • large mixing bowl • small
mixing bowl • rubber spatula • large, round serving platter

1 With an adult's help, fill a small saucepan with water and bring it to a boil over high heat. Carefully drop in the eggs whole, and cook them for 10 minutes. Using pot holders to hold the pan's handle, drain the water without tipping the eggs out. Quickly refill the pan with cold water and ice cubes. Set eggs aside for about 10 minutes to cool completely.

2 Ask an adult to help you use a utility knife to finely chop the onion and celery. Set them aside. When the eggs have completely cooled, crack and peel them. Use a grater to finely shred the eggs. Set them aside.

3 Fill a large, heavy saucepan with water and, with an adult's help, bring it to a boil over high heat. Add the macaroni and cook according to package directions.

4 Place a colander in the sink. With an adult's help, pour out macaroni to drain. Rinse under cold water for two minutes. When macaroni has drained completely, transfer it to a large mixing bowl.

5 In a small mixing bowl, combine the mayonnaise, pickle relish, vinegar, mustard, salt, and celery seed. Use a rubber spatula to blend ingredients thoroughly. Add the food coloring a few drops at a time and stir well. When mixture turns medium gray, add it to the large mixing bowl. Stir in the onions, celery, and eggs, and gently toss until macaroni is evenly coated.

6 To mold your brain, carefully spoon the macaroni mixture onto your serving platter. Use your clean, dry hands to press the mixture into a large, oval brain. Serve immediately or cover tightly with plastic wrap and refrigerate up to three days in advance.

Serves: 12 gray-matter gobblers

Handwiches

A truly handsome finger food you can put together in a snap!

INGREDIENTS

24 slices white or wheat bread

12 slices salami

12 slices American cheese

12 slices turkey

12 slices cheddar cheese

green and black food coloring

1 small carrot, grated

½ cup mayonnaise

12 slices black olive

chopped pimientos, drained
   (about 1 tablespoon)

squeeze-top bottle of mustard

TOOLS YOU'LL NEED

• pencil • tracing paper • scissors • small serrated knife •
• mixing spoon • small bowl • small rubber spatula •
• large serving platter or individual plates

1   To start, you'll need two hand patterns—
left and right hands—big enough to fit
on your bread slices without touching the
crusts. Use your pencil and tracing paper to
sketch them out. Try making the fingers
slightly crooked at the knuckles, like craggy
old hands. Once you're happy with the
patterns, cut them out with scissors.

2   Lay one pattern over a slice of bread and, with an adult's help,
carefully cut all around the pattern with a small serrated knife.
Repeat with 11 more slices. Use the second pattern in the
same manner with the remaining 12 slices of bread. Set them
aside in two separate piles. Cut all salami and American cheese
slices in the same manner with the right-hand pattern and all
turkey and cheddar cheese slices with the left-hand pattern.
Set them aside in separate piles.

3 With a mixing spoon and small bowl, stir two drops of green food coloring and one drop of black food coloring into the mayonnaise and blend well. Mayonnaise should be a light, gangrenous gray-green. If color appears too dark, lighten it with additional mayonnaise.

4 To assemble scarred and jeweled right hands, make an assembly line in this order: right-hand bread slices, gangrenous mayonnaise, American cheese and salami slices, grated carrot, olives, pimientos, and mustard. Use the spatula to carefully spread each slice with mayonnaise. Layer with cheese, then salami on top. Line two or three carrot pieces lengthwise and about four pieces widthwise as stitches on the center of each hand. To add jewelry, push a piece of pimiento into the hole in each olive slice, then place the olive on top of each ring finger. Squirt a small dot of mustard on each fingertip as a fungal nail.

5 To assemble scab-covered left hands, make an assembly line in this order: left-hand bread slices, gangrenous mayonnaise, cheddar cheese and turkey slices, pimientos, and mustard. Use the spatula to spread each slice with mayonnaise. Layer with cheese, then turkey on top. Add several pimientos as scabs, then squirt a small dot of mustard on each fingertip. Add a few dots of gangrenous mayonnaise over some of the scabs to create blobs of pus. Arrange all open-faced sandwiches on the serving platter or individual plates. Serve immediately or cover tightly in plastic wrap and store in the refrigerator up to one day in advance.

Serves: 12 friends
who'll lend a hand—
one pair per pal

Dynamite Sticks

Guests will blow their tops over this explosively tasty side dish!

INGREDIENTS

3 medium-sized bananas
(straighter ones work best)

½ lemon

3 cups water, divided

6-ounce package red gelatin, such
as cherry Jell-O®

6 red, orange, or yellow gumdrops

6 chow mein noodles

Stove top

TOOLS YOU'LL NEED

• paring knife • 2 medium mixing bowls • medium saucepan
• pot holders • large spoon • 6 empty 6-ounce frozen juice concentrate cardboard cans • serving plates • can opener (not electric)

1 With an adult's help, peel the bananas and slice them in half widthwise with the paring knife. Place them into a mixing bowl and squeeze juice from the lemon over the bananas to prevent them from turning brown. Set aside.

2 With an adult's help, bring 2 cups water (plus a bit extra to allow for evaporation) to boil in a saucepan. Using pot holders, pour 2 cups boiling water into a second mixing bowl. Pour in the gelatin and stir well with a large spoon to dissolve gelatin completely. Pour in 1 cup very cold water and stir. Place mixing bowl in the refrigerator for about 15 minutes to thicken slightly.

3 To assemble the dynamite sticks, place a spoonful of slightly thickened gelatin into each empty 6-ounce can, the firecracker mold. Insert one banana half into each can with the flat, cut

66

portion down. Center each banana in the can so that it does not hit the sides. Also, the banana should not extend beyond the can's rim, so trim off any excess. Spoon the remaining gelatin evenly into the cans. Place the cans in the refrigerator for about three hours or until gelatin is firm.

4 Meanwhile, to create flaming dynamite wicks, wedge one gumdrop onto each chow mein noodle. Set aside.

5 When the dynamite sticks are firm, take them out of the refrigerator. Dip each can up to the rim in warm water for about 30 seconds. Do not allow the water to touch the gelatin dynamite stick. Then invert each can onto individual serving plates. With an adult's help, use a can opener to poke a small hole into the bottom of the juice can. The dynamite sticks will easily slide out onto the plates. You can make your dynamite sticks up to one week in advance and store, tightly covered, in plastic wrap in the refrigerator. Do not remove dynamite sticks from their molds until you're ready to serve.

6 Insert one gumdrop wick into each dynamite stick and serve.

Serves: 6 explosive personalities

PUTRID PRESENTATION

Tape several inflated balloons underneath the table where guests will be eating and hide a large safety pin nearby. As guests cut into their dynamite, slide your hand under the table and explode a balloon!

Bad Breath Biscuits

Here's a smelly dish fit for all your bad breath buddies!

INGREDIENTS

12-ounce jar fire-roasted red bell
  peppers, packed in oil
6 slices bologna
¼ cup butter
¾ cup cornmeal
¾ cup flour
2 teaspoons baking powder

½ teaspoon salt
1 egg
⅔ cup milk
¼ cup sugar
1½ cups fresh frozen whole-kernel
  corn, thawed on paper towels,
  divided

Oven and Microwave/Stove top

TOOLS YOU'LL NEED

• cutting board • paring knife • pot holders • large mixing bowl
• whisk • small mixing bowl • small ladle
• 12-capacity muffin tray, well greased • wire rack

1 Open and drain the peppers and lay them on a cutting board. With an adult's help, use your paring knife to carve out 12 pairs of lips. Make each one wide enough to cover the top of a muffin without hanging over. Set them aside.

2 To prepare coated tongues, cut the bologna circles in half-moon shapes using a paring knife. (Always ask an adult to help you when using a knife.) Next, cut the sides off of each slice to create a natural-looking tongue shape with a rounded tip. Set aside.

3 Ask an adult to help you preheat the oven to 400 degrees. Place butter into a microwave-safe liquid-measuring cup.

Place it in the microwave on high (100%) for about 20 seconds or until completely melted. (Butter may also be melted in a small saucepan on your stove top.) With an adult's help, use pot holders to remove the butter from the microwave and set aside.

4 Pour the cornmeal, flour, baking powder, and salt into a large mixing bowl. Gently stir using a whisk. Crack the egg in a small mixing bowl and whisk together with the milk and sugar until thoroughly combined. Pour the egg mixture into the cornmeal mixture. Stir in the melted butter and 1 cup thawed, drained corn. (Reserve the rest for making rotten teeth.)

5 With a small ladle, divide the biscuit batter into the well-greased muffin cups. Then lay one pair of lips over the top of each biscuit, parted enough to fit a row of rotten corn teeth and a tongue as shown.

6 With an adult's help, place the biscuits in the oven and bake for 15 to 18 minutes or until biscuits turn golden. With pot holders, carefully remove biscuits from oven and place the tray on a wire rack to cool slightly before serving. Bad Breath Biscuits can be made up to two weeks in advance and stored, frozen, in a tightly sealed container. (Lay biscuits flat—do not stack them in the freezer.) A few hours before serving, place them in the refrigerator to thaw. To warm biscuits before serving, arrange them on a foil-lined baking sheet. Cover them lightly with a second layer of foil, and heat at 350 degrees for about 10 minutes or until warmed through.

Serves: 12 odor eaters

BEASTLY
BEVERAGES

**Bubbling
Battery Acid**
(page 80)

**Body-Part
Punch**
(page 7?)

**Buggy
Eyeballs**
(page 78)

OPTOMETRY
DEPARTMENT

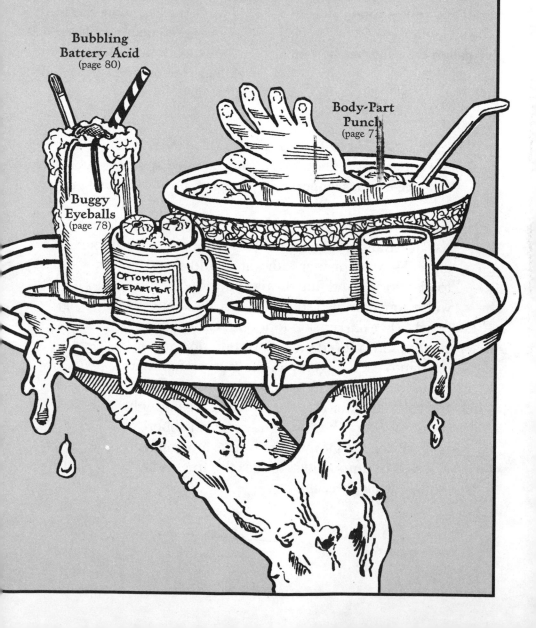

Body-Part Punch

Give yourself a hand—this punch looks like hard work, but it's not. And your friends are sure to give you a standing ovation.

INGREDIENTS

red and yellow food coloring
5 red gumdrops
½ gallon lime sherbet, softened

1 large package lime-flavored presweetened, powdered drink mix, such as Koolaid®
2 liters lemon-lime soda, well chilled

TOOLS YOU'LL NEED

• new rubber glove • pitcher • long-handled spoon • rubber band
• ice-cream scooper • large punch bowl • ladle • cups

1 You'll need to prepare your floating body part at least a day in advance. First, thoroughly rinse out your rubber glove. Fill your pitcher with water. Add one drop red food coloring and one drop yellow food coloring. Stir with a long-handled spoon. The color should be light peach. (For darker skin tones use chocolate milk rather than colored water.) Wedge one gumdrop into each fingertip of the glove. Then have someone hold the glove open while you pour the colored water into the glove. Leave enough room to secure the end tightly with a rubber band. Place the glove in the freezer overnight. For ease in unmolding, be sure the fingers lay straight while freezing.

2 Clear enough space in your refrigerator to fit the punch bowl. About one hour before you're ready to serve the punch, scoop the softened sherbet into the punch bowl and add the powdered drink mix. Stir together using the long-handled spoon and refrigerate.

3 Just before serving, remove the glove from the freezer. Peel the glove off the hand. You may need to run it under warm water to help loosen the glove. Take the sherbet mixture out of the refrigerator and put the frozen hand in it. Add the chilled lemon-lime soda, stir well, and serve.

Serves: About 12 body slammers

PUTRID PRESENTATION

To make each glass especially disgusting, serve with a few Toenail Trimmings (see page 32).

Pesticide Punch

This punch may paralyze any insect pests, but it will leave your bug-crazed buddies buzzing for more!

INGREDIENTS

12 Gummi Fish®
6 black mini jelly beans
6 Gummi Worms®
6 fizzing drink tablets, such as Fizzies® Instant Sparkling Drink Tablets, any flavor

1 quart lemon-lime soda, well chilled
1 quart blue-colored sports drink, such as Gatorade® Cool Blue Raspberry, well chilled
1 cup chocolate jimmie sprinkles

TOOLS YOU'LL NEED

• 2 ice cube trays • large reclosable plastic bag •
• rolling pin • large pitcher • long-handled spoon •
• tall glasses • iced-tea spoons •

1 You'll need to prepare your dead fish and bugs the day before you plan to serve them. Place one fish, headfirst, in each of the 12 openings in one ice cube tray. It's okay if tails hang outside the tray. Fill the other tray with six black jelly beans on one side and six Gummi Worms on the other. Let the worms' excess length hang over the sides. Slowly fill each tray with water and freeze overnight.

2 Place the fizzing drink tablets into a large reclosable bag. Remove excess air and seal the bag. To crush the tablets into pesticide powder, firmly roll the rolling pin back and forth over the bag until tablets are finely ground. Set aside.

74

3 In a large pitcher, mix together the lemon-lime soda and sports drink with a long-handled spoon.

4 To assemble, place about 2 tablespoons jimmie sprinkles into the bottom of each glass as a sandy layer. Empty the ice cube trays and fill each glass with a dead fish, a bug, and a second dead fish, and top with a worm. Be sure the worm dangles over the glass's rim.

5 *Slowly* fill each glass with the blue soda mixture. Just before you serve this toxic treat, stir in a teaspoon of pesticide powder using individual iced-tea spoons and watch it fizz! If you'd like to get a head start on this deadly drink, you can do steps 1 and 2 two to three weeks in advance. Then, on the day of your party, follow steps 3 through 5.

Serves: 6 party bugs

Bowl o' Bile

Don't lose your lunch—save it! A bowl brimming with projectile punch adds a gutsy flair to any gastronomic get-together!

INGREDIENTS

3 cups water, divided

3 medium-sized ripe
bananas, peeled

1 cup sugar

12-ounce can frozen orange
juice concentrate, thawed

¾ cup frozen lemonade
concentrate, thawed

3 cups unsweetened pineapple
juice

3 liters lemon-lime soda,
well chilled

1 cup mini marshmallows

TOOLS YOU'LL NEED

• large punch bowl (one that can be frozen) • blender •
long-handled spoon • plastic wrap •
potato masher • ladle • cups

1 Clear enough room in your freezer to fit the punch bowl. Place the punch bowl on your work surface.

2 Place 1 cup water, the bananas, and the sugar into a blender. With an adult's help, blend on medium speed until bananas are smooth but slightly chunky, about 15 to 20 seconds.

3 Pour banana mixture into punch bowl and add orange juice concentrate, lemonade concentrate, pineapple juice, and remaining 2 cups water. Stir well with a long-handled spoon. Wrap the bowl tightly in plastic wrap and freeze two to three hours or overnight. You can freeze this bile mixture up to one week in advance of your party.

4 Remove your bowl of bile from the freezer about two hours before guests arrive. Just before serving, mash bile to a chunky consistency using a potato masher. Note: If your punch bowl is made of glass, use extra caution and have an adult hold the bowl steady while you break up the bile. Pour in the chilled soda and mini marshmallows (bile chunks), stir, and serve.

Serves: About 24 stomach pumpers

PUTRID PRESENTATION

Peel the label off an empty bottle of liquid antacid and attach it to a clean glass bottle. Fill it with whole milk and color it Pepto-Bismol® pink using red food coloring. As guests are sipping your retched-up refreshment, offer them a spoonful of your stomach-soothing medication.

Buggy Eyeballs

Bugged-out, bulging eyeballs are the eye-deal adornment for this oozing warm beverage!

INGREDIENTS

16 large marshmallows
16 black jelly beans
red food coloring
½ gallon milk

8 1-ounce envelopes hot cocoa mix
½ cup creamy peanut butter
1 can whipped topping

Stove top

TOOLS YOU'LL NEED

• **kitchen scissors** • **16 red-and-white striped straws** • **small saucer**
• **toothpick** • **large saucepan** • **wooden spoon** • **8 mugs**

1 With the scissors, trim each straw so that it extends about 2 inches beyond the rim of a mug. Snip an *X* into the tall side portion of each marshmallow, cutting about halfway into each. Wedge one jelly bean into the opening. Gently squeeze the marshmallow around the jelly bean to form a beady black eye. Repeat with the remaining marshmallows.

2 Carefully wedge one straw into the bottom of each marshmallow eyeball a little more than halfway in. Squirt several drops of red food coloring into a small saucer.

3 Dip the tip of a toothpick into the food coloring, then drag it randomly over the marshmallow to create veins. Repeat this several times, crossing over the veins so that the eyes appear bloodshot. Repeat with the remaining marshmallow eyeballs. (You can prepare Buggy Eyeballs up to two days in advance and store them, loosely covered, at room temperature until you're ready to garnish your beverage.)

4 Just before serving, pour the milk into a large saucepan. With an adult's help, heat the milk over medium heat, stirring constantly with a wooden spoon. When milk is very warm but not boiling, stir in the packets of cocoa mix and peanut butter. Continue stirring over low heat until all ingredients are thoroughly mixed.

5 Line up the mugs on your work surface. Ask an adult to help you evenly pour the cocoa mixture into the mugs. Place two Buggy Eyeballs in each mug and top with a squirt of whipped topping. Serve immediately.

Serves: 8 peeper poppers

PUTRID PRESENTATION

Add an elegant flair for all the female eyeball eaters on your guest list! Insert eyelashes (tiny snips of black shoelace licorice) into the top of each pair of girl's eyeballs.

Bubbling Battery Acid

Look what dear old Dad dragged in from the garage—an old, corroded battery, just oozing its juices. Drink up!

INGREDIENTS

1 quart chocolate ice cream

½ cup strawberry-flavored syrup

1 quart milk

yellow food coloring

1 quart seltzer water, well chilled

8 ropes each red and black licorice

TOOLS YOU'LL NEED

• 8 tall glasses • ice-cream scooper • iced-tea spoons • blender

1 Evenly divide the ice cream into the tall glasses with the ice-cream scooper. Place one iced-tea spoon into each glass.

2 Pour the syrup and milk into a blender. Then, with an adult's help, blend on medium speed for about five seconds. Add four or five drops of yellow food coloring per serving and the chilled seltzer, and blend again for five seconds.

3 Quickly pour the seltzer mixture into the glasses and serve while the battery acid is still bubbling and foaming. Dangle a rope of red licorice for the positive charge and a rope of black licorice for the negative charge over each glass.

Serves: 8 maniac mechanics